The Quick Reference Guide

This is a condensed, light, paperback version of Purna Asatti: A Roadmap To A Better Life Through Complete Connection. It is intended to give you just the basics of each stage and the background on where it all came from. To keep things small, this version does not include the art or poetry for each stage. For more detailed exercises and the practical how-to for each task, the art and poetry for each stage and the full experience of the original book, please see the full, hardback print version of the book at
KathrynColleen.com

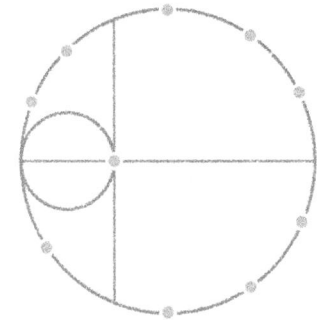

Purna Asatti

(Sanskrit: Complete Connection)

Quick Reference Guide

Amy Kathryn Colleen Messegee, PhD

Trend Factor Press

Trend Factor Press, a division of Sparticle Concepts LLC
1530 P B Lane #M4819, Wichita Falls, TX 76302-2612
KathrynColleen.com

Copyright © 2019 by Amy Kathryn Colleen Messegee, PhD.
All rights reserved.

This content is protected by United States and International copyright laws. No part of this content may be reproduced or distributed without the written consent of the author.

ISBN-13 978-0-9818669-5-6
(Paperback and ePub, English)

This book has an accompanying full edition, music album, podcast, multiple translations, and many extra resources. To contact the author, or to find more information about this book, translations, other publications, podcasts and music, please visit KathrynColleen.com. Your thoughts and questions are welcomed.

Guide

Where This Roadmap Came From	6
How To Use This Book	7
Resources	8
Your Destination Is Unique.... The Road To Get There Is NOT	11
What You Get When You Put It All Together - The Cycle Of Human Development	14
The Key To Your Journey - CONNECTION	17
The Symbol - Something To Help You Focus On Connection	18
A Private Journey	20
Before You Begin - Physical, Mental And Financial Safety	22
Let's Go!	23
Stage One: Everything Is Me	24
Stage Two: I Am Everything Except Experiences And Reflexes	28
Stage Three: I Am My Needs	32
Stage Four: Others Have Needs Too	36
Stage Five: I Am My Value Set / Ideology / Religion / Beliefs	40
Stage Six: To Each Their Own	44
Stage Seven: Questioning Everything	50
Stage Eight: I Am A Child Of The Universe / Divine	56
Stage Nine: I Am A Consciousness Trapped In This Body	60
Stage Ten: I Am The ONE Consciousness	64
Stage Eleven: I Am The One Consciousness And The Physical Manifestation Simultaneously And There Is No Difference	68
Questions, Answers And Additional Resources	74
About The Author	75

Where This Roadmap Came From

I was 31 when I woke up. I remember it vividly. I looked in the mirror like I had been asleep in the car and someone else had driven us into a ditch. I did not like where things were going physically or financially, or career-wise and I felt like there was something really important that I was completely clueless about. I wanted to take the journey that so many others had taken - the journey of self-development and self-understanding towards a more fulfilling life. This journey has taken more than a decade of walking through some of the worst and best times in my life. What I wish I had back then, was a roadmap. I wish I had something to guide me on what to do first, and what to do next, and the next step after that, etc. If I had been handed a roadmap to self-development back then, I might have gotten to this point a LOT sooner and with a lot less pain. Perhaps twelve years could have been more like one or two and many mistakes and wasted effort could have been avoided. If I had a roadmap, I might have been able to get quickly to my purpose, and a life of peace and joy. So **this roadmap is for you**. May it guide you on your journey and speed you to where you want to be, wherever that is.

This roadmap is the result of aggregating the research and writings of more than fifty scholars, researchers, authors, speakers, and thought leaders over that twelve year period. It stands on the shoulders of giants to distill their findings and influence into a single coherent roadmap that accelerates your self-understanding. It is a process and a practice for keeping you in the beautiful states of your choosing through complete connection to yourself and every aspect of your life.

"If I had been handed a roadmap back then, I might have gotten to this point a LOT sooner and with a lot less pain."

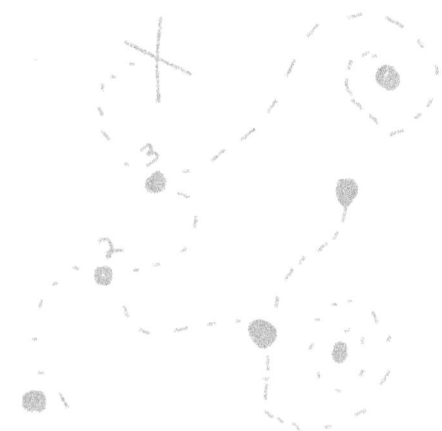

How To Use This Quick Reference

This book is a roadmap for self-understanding through complete connection. It guides you through eleven stages, each with tasks, recommended resources and questions to spark your thinking. Work through each task starting from Stage One. When you complete the roadmap, you can read parts of it again and repeat exercises to help keep you in the stages you want experience most.

Although it is simple, it may not be easy... This journey will not be instant. Depending on where you are now, you may have significant baggage to unpack and you may have major mistakes to correct. Your circle of friends and family may change dramatically. If you are with the wrong person, you are about to find out. If you are in the wrong career, that too is about to become clear. That dissatisfaction you feel is based in your soul and to feel the kind of peace that you seek, you will need to face the realities of your past choices and start consciously making better ones.

If you are lucky, perhaps you are not too far off the mark. But even if you are with the right person and in the right career, this journey is not easy. You will face yourself - your beautiful reality and your dark side. Your humanity will be laid bare for you to see and you will be challenged to love yourself, not in spite of your humanity, but because of it. **On the other side of this journey is a life so amazing and joyous; peaceful and content, that words will fail and all you will feel is gratitude for each day.**

If you currently enjoy a particular religion, you can use this process to develop a deeper level of faith. However, the path to get there includes questioning everything and growing to see your deity in a higher, more expanded role and from a less anthropomorphic perspective. Ultimately, you will come to recognize the immensity of your deity's reach and what they have gifted you.

The art in this book is there to give you another way to think about the concepts and to SLOW YOU DOWN. **The ideal pace is one stage per month**.

Work through each task starting from Stage One. Read parts again and repeat exercises to keep you in the stages you want to experience most.

Please think long and hard about whether you are ready. If you choose to proceed, you alone are responsible for what happens; good, bad, wonderful, ecstatic, amazing, terrifying, and all.

If and when you are ready, read on.

Resources

The following authors' work directly inspired or influenced this roadmap. They are listed in no particular order along with a quick note on what I learned from them. No one is more important or profound than another. Consider them important resources for your journey. Seek them out and let their writings, podcasts and other works influence you and contribute to your connections. You will see some of their specific writings and podcasts mentioned in the roadmap in each stage. Throughout your journey, you should seek as many resources from these and other authors as you are compelled to find. Let your natural curiosity lead you to the right inspiration at the right time.

Seek as many resources from these and other authors as you are compelled to find.

- Tara Brach (meditation, mindfulness, connecting to your body and reality)

- Tim Ferriss (rejecting and replacing societal rules, defining your ideal life and achieving it, questioning everything, 80/20 analysis, connecting to your body, learning languages and other skills quickly)

- Dr. Henry Cloud and Dr. John Townsend (setting healthy boundaries on your time, attention and space)

- Dr. Robert Kegan (social and moral development)

- Dr. James W. Fowler III (religious development)

- Dr. Jane Loevinger (ego development)

- Sri Aurobindo (spiritual development)

- Dr. Abraham Maslow (human development)

- Dale Carnegie (social skills)

- Dave Ramsey (financial freedom)

- Chris Thomas (decluttering your spaces)

- Margot Anand (tantric sexual practices and theory)

- KRS-One (manifesting, connecting to the Silent Observer, creating your reality)

- Spencer Johnson (facing reality and optimizing it)

- Yogani (meditation techniques, developing practice routines and the nature of dichotomy in the universe)

- Ray Dalio (developing principles)

- Richard Carlson, Ph.D. (eliminating worry)

- Don Miguel Ruiz (principles - *The Four Agreements*)
- James Altucher and Claudia Azula Altucher (standing up for yourself, protecting your time and priorities, and how to say NO.)
- Henry David Thoreau (minimalism, questioning social and societal rules and perspective on nature)
- Charlie Hoehn (eliminating stress and mild depression or anxiety)
- Ori Brafman and Rom Brafman (making better decisions)
- Elisabeth Kubler-Ross, M.D. and David Kessler (wisdom from the elderly)
- Mark Manson (not taking things so seriously and not caring what people think)
- Greg McKeown (essentialism)
- Patrick Rhone (minimalism and being satisfied with what you have)
- Rolf Potts (travel and releasing yourself from societal rules)
- Steven Pressfield (the process of creativity and defeating the negative voice)
- Jon Kabat-Zinn (mindfulness and meditation)
- Elle Luna (exploring purpose)
- Wim Hof (breathing techniques and controlling immune and emotional response)
- Eckhart Tolle (connecting to the moment)
- Robert Lanza, MD (effect of human consciousness on the universe)
- Steven Weinberg (the science of the first three minutes post Big Bang)
- Tony Robbins (self mastery)
- Gabriel Wyner (language learning and efficient memorization)
- Jordan Harbinger (social interaction and starting over after crisis)
- Robert Greene (the true nature of humanity in all stages)
- His Holiness The Dalai Lama (compassion and oneness)
- Father Thomas Merton (spiritual and religious development)
- Father Thomas Keating (spiritual and religious development)
- Judith Orloff M.D. (connecting to intuition and the body)

- Joe Navarro (dangerous personalities found in stages three and five)

- Pamela Miles (Reiki)

- Ryan Holiday (connecting to challenges and overcoming ego)

- Marcus Aurelius (stoicism)

- Seneca The Younger (stoicism)

- Simon Sinek (human nature and motivation)

- Religious Texts (the nature of humanity, life and the universe):

  - The Bible

  - The Torah

  - The Tao Te Ching

  - The Vedas

  - The Qur'an

  - The Bhagavad Gita

  - The Dhammapada

Your Destination Is Unique ...
The Road To Get There Is NOT

Reflecting on my own journey, I wondered if what I went through was unique. I found it was not at all unique. I found that many before me had documented stages of human development and suggested a series of stages that we all go through. Kegan documented social stages. Fowler documented religious stages. Loevinger documented ego stages. Then I did my own digging around. Clearly, people like the Dalai Lama, Mother Theresa, Gandhi, Mandela, and other significant figures had gotten much farther. What were their additional stages? In the end, I found that **each of these sets of stages had significant overlap and linked up nicely to form a single coherent cyclical path of development.** Let's look at the pieces.

Each of us here in the human experience develops along the same path from birth.

Although your hopes and dreams and the life you ultimately want to craft for yourself are completely unique to you, what you are experiencing right now in your desire for self-development is not unique. You are in great company. Each of us here in the human experience develops along the same path from birth.

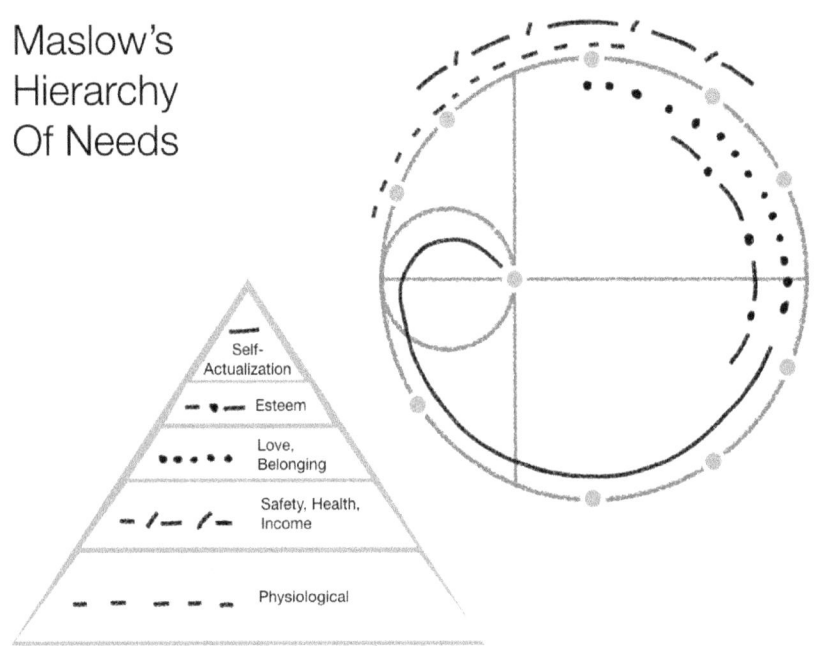

Maslow's Hierarchy of Needs showed how we develop from the point of view of our priorities. It maps into stages of development as seen here. Maslow's physiological needs correspond to stages two through four, safety, health and income correspond to stages three through five. Love and belonging are found in stages four through six, and so on.

The Chakra System

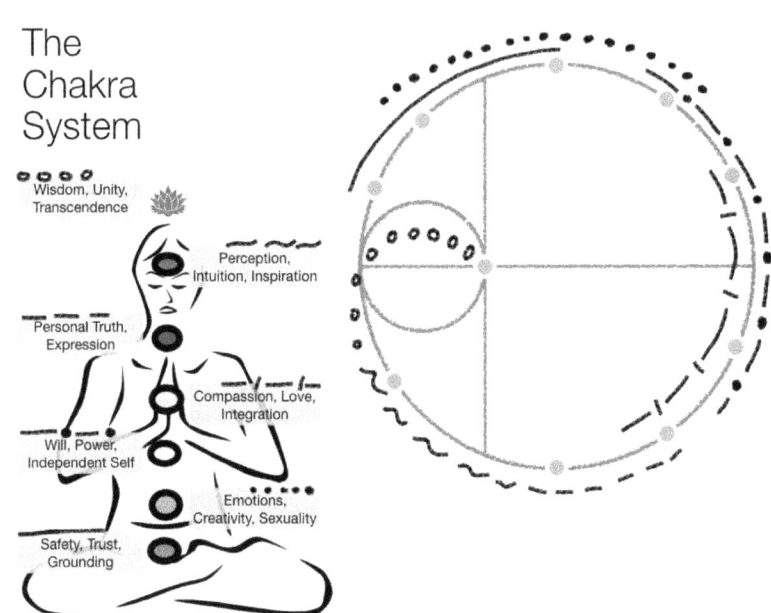

Chakras are energy centers throughout the body thought to be linked to specific concepts like safety, compassion, expression, etc. The chakras also map to Maslow's hierarchy and to a development process as seen here. Notice we are working from the ground up.

Many other psychologists and thought leaders had similar ideas, each detailing portions of a larger cycle of development. Seen here are just a few of the more prominent names and where their work fits in.

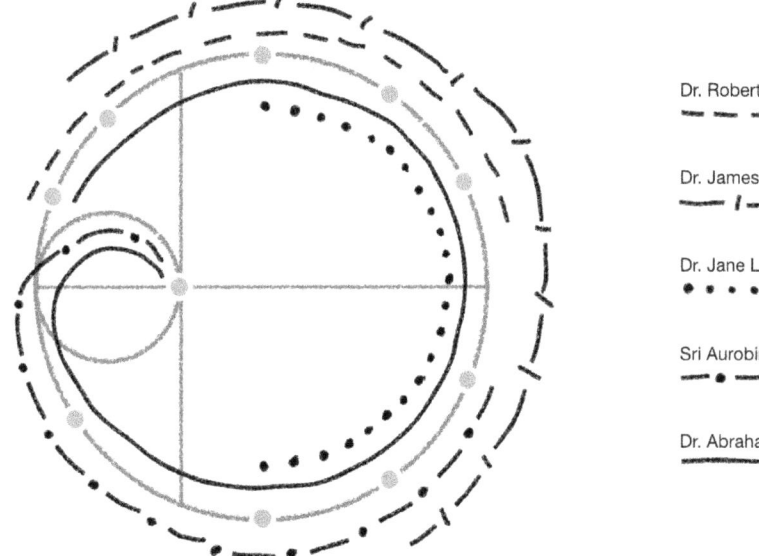

Dr. Robert Kegan

Dr. James Fowler III

Dr. Jane Loevinger

Sri Aurobindo

Dr. Abraham Maslow

We see specific themes within their work that suggest four distinct phases of this cycle. We begin by becoming aware of ourselves, then we become aware of others and their ideas and we compare ourselves to them. We then transition to unifying those ideas, and lastly to unifying ourselves.

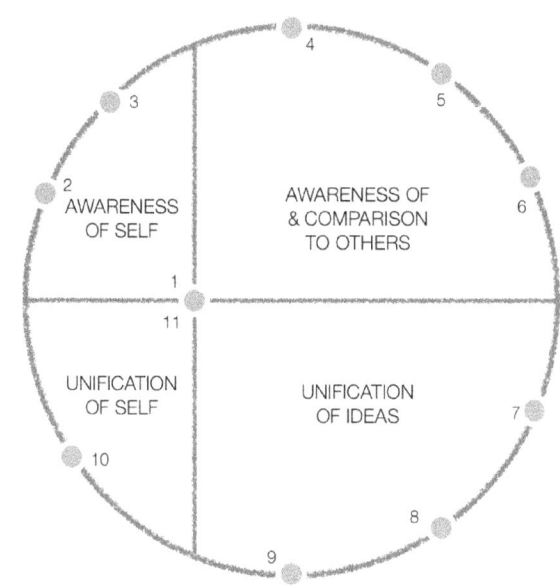

What You Get When You Put It All Together - The Cycle of Human Development

There are eleven stages of development that you CAN experience. (That does not guarantee you will.)

Almost everyone wakes up at some point in their lives (usually between stages five and six). Some call it a midlife crisis, or a quarter-life crisis. Some people wake up much later and some not at all. Some wake up and decide to not take the journey and essentially go back to sleep. Earlier stages are not lesser; in fact, they are essential and must be completed, or you will keep being pulled back into them again and again. The large majority of people in the western world do not make it past stages five or six and spend most of their days there, happily enough.

There are eleven stages of development that you CAN experience; picking up the pieces and completing stages as we revisit them again and again over the course of our lives.

These eleven stages are not a staircase or a straight line of milestones to be achieved. They are not a race for achievement. They are a circle - a cycle of human development that we traverse over and over, trying to pick up the pieces and complete stages as we revisit them again and again over the course of our lives. **Even as you spend more time in later stages, you will periodically be pulled back to earlier stages by major life events** (injury, family issues, elections, etc). You cannot avoid coming around the cycle again and again. But you can spend a lot less time in these earlier stages where life is hard and negative emotions dominate; and you can spend a lot

You might ...

(1) work through the tasks, and then

(2) enjoy the recommended reading and podcasts, and then

(3) answer the questions to fuel your thinking.

more time in later stages where life is easy, joyous, fulfilling and peaceful.

Stage one and stage eleven are essentially the same (with some added richness). **The irony that we enter this world with the right idea and then must work our way back to it, is rather funny.** The universe has a sense of humor.

Ask yourself: which stage do you find yourself in most of the time? As you go through your day, try to step back from yourself and see where you are on this cycle. Some days, you might traverse the entire cycle in one day. Other days might find you specifically in one stage or another.

Based on the stage where you tend to spend the most time, you have some work to do. **Each stage has a set of important tasks** that must be addressed and questions that you can use to help complete that stage and move yourself to the next. If you leave something undone in one stage, you can be guaranteed that life will bring you back there again soon to keep working. So be proactive yet patient about it and try to complete each stage's tasks as you go.

It is most efficient to start from the beginning and pick up any pieces you have left undone in earlier stages. Most adults wake up between stages five and six, but have significant tasks still to do from stages one through four. Leaving these tasks undone means you will be pulled back to these stages instead of moving forward. It will delay your development. So start at Stage One.

What follows is a roadmap for each stage's characteristics, tasks, recommended reading and some helpful questions. **It helps to keep a journal (on paper or otherwise) to track your thinking and progress.** There are nuances to these tasks so it is worth reading as much material from as many authors as you can to help you in each stage. To that end, There are recommended books in each stage that I have personally found helpful. You should also seek out other books, blogs, and podcasts to give you as much perspective as possible. The key is to read the right books and do the right exercises, asking the right questions, at the right point in the cycle. But if you find that a different order to things works better for you, do not hesitate to make your own best method.

The Key To Your Journey - CONNECTION

Now that we have the cycle and we understand a bit about the stages, the big question is HOW do we move from one stage to another? HOW do we efficiently, effectively and permanently shift perspectives? What is the catalyst that makes someone go from one stage to the next?

The answer to all of those questions is: CONNECTION. Connection means many things. It means being present with, acknowledging, taking ownership of, responsibility for, and forming a deep relationship with the thing in question.

Progressing from one stage to another, or remaining in later stages is a matter of connecting to some aspect of yourself, others, your life, your money, your purpose, your body, your thoughts, ... IN THE RIGHT ORDER. In the roadmap that follows, specific tasks and exercises will guide you through exactly how to do that.

If you focus on forming and maintaining connection, your evolution through the stages will happen on its own. Just focus on connection.

Connection means being present with, acknowledging, taking ownership of, responsibility for, and forming a deep relationship with the thing in question.

The Symbol - Something To Help You Focus On Connection

The symbol developed for this process is based on the four quarters mentioned above, on the eleven stages, the uniqueness of stages one and eleven, and on the many beautiful religious symbols in the world today. You can easily find your favorite symbol inside this one, from the Christian cross to the Muslim moon. You can draw the Star of David between the points or just as easily connect the dots to make the Buddhist symbol for Om. It provides a simple, beautiful, unified symbol that helps you chart your path, remember important lessons, and stay on track. Connect your religion to this symbol to increase your commitment, or meditate on the symbol to set your intentions with or without religion. It has so many uses, you are sure to find a way to use it that suits your journey specifically and accelerates your efforts. It comes in many variations and you can even make your own version. Seen here are just a few variations that have been useful reminders for myself and my students. Simply seeing the symbol can remind you to spend this day in a beautiful state, connect more deeply with others or just honor your commitment to yourself to go to the gym. Use it in any way it may serve you.

 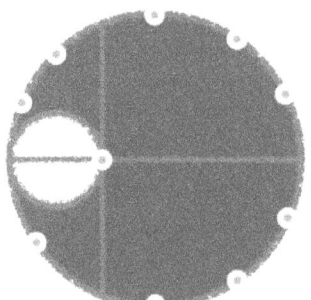 

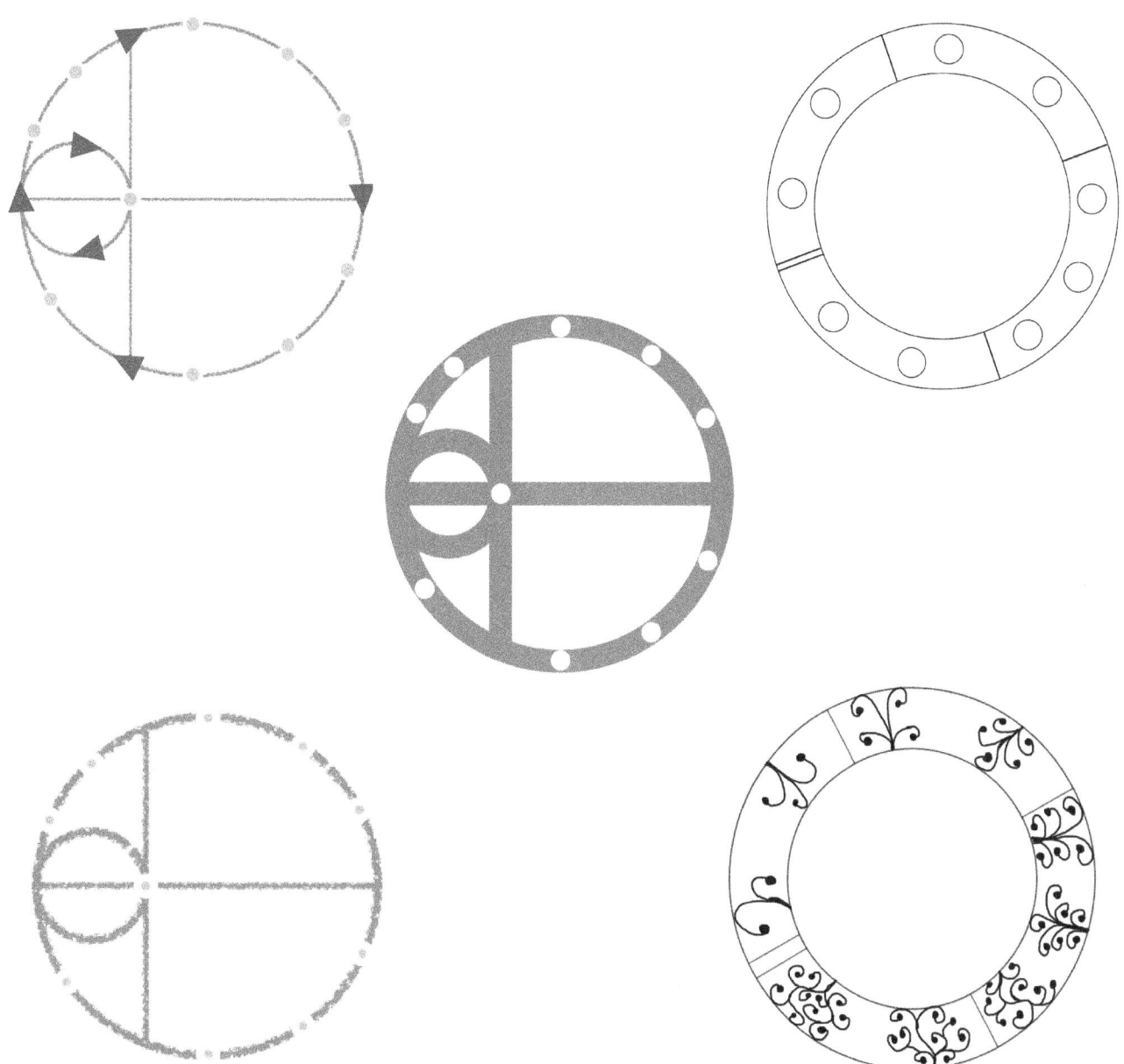

A Private Journey

Your personal journey of self discovery is a critical life long pursuit. It is one of the most profound efforts you will ever undertake. Periodically, it will occupy your whole being. Ironically, or perhaps in perfect balance... nobody cares. The reality is that nobody cares about your journey as they are much too wrapped up in their own equally profound self discovery and rediscovery.

That is great news because it means there is nothing you can really "discover" about your temporary little self that will be all that big of a deal to anyone. For those that know you, they probably already saw in you what you just figured out. And for those who don't know you, they just do not care. So be who you like, do what you want, be who you want - it doesn't matter! That's freedom!

But it gets better… **The journey of self discovery is so critical because it is critical to reach the ultimate and most important conclusion about yourself - that THERE IS NO SELF.**

We spend decades labeling our selves, crafting our selves, honing self images and self presentations. While certainly a fun amusement, these crafted selves serve as little more than adaptations, They help us navigate our present situation socially, politically and financially and understand our current place in the world.

We peel the onion of our "true selves"; celebrating each layer we find and declaring anew that this layer is our true self… no, THIS LAYER is my true self. No, wait. THIS ONE! Until one day when we reach the vacant center and realize that our true self is no-self. Or more precisely, our true self is THE ONENESS - that oneness that is in all of us; not a separate self.

In that moment it strikes us that the "self" as we have been trying to define it for so very long is just a series of temporary manifestations; fleeting costumes tried on and evolved.

If we look around us we will see that everyone else that we have been trying to label and judge and identify is just exactly like us: wholly occupied by peeling away each temporary layer of self to vehemently defend the layer below.

If we look around us we will see that everyone else that we have been trying to label and judge and identify is just exactly like us: wholly occupied by peeling away each temporary layer of self to vehemently defend the layer below. Each of us, however, eventually arrives at the reality in our own time; some not until their last day on this Earth, and some much younger.

We wake up to a world where we are no longer trapped in the need to define a temporary self for ourselves or anyone else. We are at last free to really look around us, no longer occupied by the futile pursuit of what does not even exist - your self. We wake up to the freedom to pursue making a difference, or making something beautiful, or making someone happy... or any number of things that bring joy to the oneness inside us and others.

But this is a private journey; each of us to ourselves. Please do not be disappointed if others are not mesmerized by your journey. They are too busy with their own. This can make you feel isolated in your journey. But at the same moment, everyone you see is on the exact same journey. If you can find others actively working this roadmap, they may be a community of support and resources for you. When you reach later stages, you will be delighted to find that others in those same later stages will love to hear about your journey and you will love to hear about theirs. There is deep personal connection down this road. So fear not, you are never alone, and will find yourself in great community on the other side of Stage Seven.

Before You Begin - Physical, Mental and Financial Safety

Establish your own safety. **If you are not in a safe environment physically, mentally or financially, you need to change that immediately.**

If you are being abused physically or mentally, be it verbal or emotional or psychological, GET HELP NOW. Do a bit of planning to take your children and yourself to a safe environment. Take all the money and other necessities you can manage and GO. You may think at this moment that you are not strong enough, but you are. We all are. You have no idea how beautiful life can be on the other side of your fear. Please contact family, friends, the police as needed, local organizations or even your doctor (any doctor for that matter). All of these people can help you get out and establish a safe environment where you can craft a beautiful life without fear.

If your finances are a mess, gather a small emergency fund as fast as possible; just enough to handle a major car repair. Sell everything, get a second job (or a third) but make this happen FAST before you begin this process. Why? Because self development is next to impossible when you live in fear of the next car repair or other financial issue. This is Dave Ramsey's "baby step #1." It puts you more at ease while you get the rest of your life together (finance and all).

You have no idea how beautiful life can be on the other side of your fear.

LET'S GO!

Once you have established physical, mental and financial basic safety, you are ready to get started. **Start from Stage One and work through any tasks and questions that you have not already done, any that you have not done in a long time, and any that you think you could do better.** Take your time. Contemplate these questions and concepts. Give them time to evolve you. If you do the tasks, and really think about the results, you will see immediate progress. Track it in your journal.

Stage One: Everything Is Me

Characteristics

- A newborn infant (open).
- Other people are not separate from you.
- Your experiences define you.

Challenges

When you are in this stage, you can tend to obsess over the stories of your past and present; times when you were wronged. You can tend to focus on describing your current situation (for the story you will tell about it later), rather than making conscious choices about what you want your situation to be and taking action to change it. You can also feel overwhelmed at the journey ahead of you.

Tasks

Grounding Yourself...

☐ Declutter your schedule, your attention and your spaces to focus on this process.

☐ Choose a form of meditation or prayer. Set aside some time each day and hold it sacred.

Learning To Trust...

☐ Understand the emotional roots of your choices.

☐ Learn to trust yourself .

☐ Learn to trust the Universe/River/Divine.

Resources

- *Radical Acceptance* by Tara Brach
- *Deep Meditation* by Yogani
- *You Have Too Much Shit* by Chris Thomas
- *The Power of No* by James Altucher and Claudia Azula Altucher
- *Essentialism* by Greg McKeown
- *Enough* by Patrick Rhone

Questions To Fuel Your Thinking

- What experiences have shaped you? In what ways?

- What did you learn from these experiences? About yourself, about others, about the world, about life? Do you think these lessons are true?

- Was there a time when you acted out of reflex? Are you the human animal that acted? Or the witness inside?

- Within each of these experiences, consider each person involved - can you see their humanity? (if not, it's OK...).

- Within each of your experiences, can you see YOUR humanity? What were the emotional roots of your choices and actions? Be honest. How did it turn out?

- Can you see that you are not your experiences?

Stage Two: I Am Everything Except Experiences And Reflexes

Characteristics

- A young infant or child (open, learning, new)
- Impulsive
- A sense of the universe or divine as generally safe or unsafe

Challenges

In this stage, you can tend to neglect your needs by simply not knowing what they are. Traumatic events and major life experiences can pull you back to this stage as you try to process what has occurred and detach from it. That takes real effort and your needs can sometimes be neglected because they may have changed.

TASKS

Connect to experiences...

☐ Manifest the experiences you want, understanding that they teach you but are not you.

☐ Don't waste time on the past, except to see how far you have come and to be thankful for that.

Connect to your needs...

☐ Evolve your list of needs as you learn about yourself and grow. Keep this list of needs somewhere close so you can refer to it.

Connect to your body...

☐ Ensure that you are getting enough sleep.

☐ Make time for regenerative activities such as hot baths, time alone, massage, exercise, meditation or prayer, etc.

☐ Start moving. Choose a form of movement and engage with it most days.

> **RESOURCES**
>
> - *Boundaries* by Dr. Henry Cloud and Dr. John Townsend

Questions To Fuel Your Thinking

- What kind of experiences do you want in the future?

- Do you see the universe / your deity as safe or unsafe? Why?

- What are your needs? List them out: physical, nutritional, mental, emotional, intellectual, spiritual, financial, etc.

- Do you really need that? Or are you afraid of something? Why do you need that? Dig deep.

Stage Three: I Am My Needs

Characteristics

- Focused on what you perceive as your needs: food, sleep, attention, sex, money, etc.
- Other people are not individuals with needs but reflexes you can bring to bear to fulfill your own needs.
- Religion is learned through stories, experiences, images and people. Sense is made of religion based on how it can help fulfill your needs; what it can do for you.

Challenges

This is a very self-focused stage where you need to defend and fulfill your needs. However, it can be a stage where others are neglected as the collateral damage of your self-focused efforts. This can lead to alienating friends and family. It can turn you into a self-centered jerk that no one wants to be around. You must find a way to balance the fulfillment of your needs without using others and without disregarding the fact that they have needs too. This stage is very common in children and some young adults. Crisis, injury, surgery, and other medical issues will easily draw you back to this stage at any age. Because it is so self-focused, this stage is a great time to start examining your baggage from past relationships and childhood as well as an ideal stage to get out of debt (or at least start that process).

Tasks

☐ **Connect to your sexuality.**

☐ **Connect to the humanity of others** through their needs.

☐ **Connect with yourself** beyond your needs.

☐ As you realize that you are not your needs, but you HAVE needs, don't forget that you still need to attend to your needs. Although they are not you, if you do not attend to them, you can easily fall into spending extra time in this stage.

☐ **Connect with your internal energy and feelings.**

☐ **Connect with your money** - eliminate the chains of debt servitude from your life.

> ## Resources
>
> - *How to Win Friends and Influence People* by Dale Carnegie
> - *Total Money Makeover* by Dave Ramsey
> - *Love, Sex and Awakening* by Margot Anand

Questions To Fuel Your Thinking

- Are you nothing but your need for food, etc? Are you nothing but your need for sex? Do you have something else to offer this world?

- If you are not your needs, what are you?

- What are you feeling?

- What baggage do you have from childhood?

- What limiting beliefs did you pick up from your parents that may be wrong for you?

- What baggage do you have from past relationships?

- What limiting beliefs did you pick up along the way that may need to be replaced?

- What is your baggage signal? How do you know when you have just triggered your baggage? (Yelling, anger, crying, shutting down, something else?)

Stage Four: Others Have Needs Too (I Am My Needs And Others Are Their Needs)

Characteristics

- You see others as individuals with needs of their own; it is not their job to fulfill your needs.
- You practice prioritizing your needs above or below others, and others above or below each other.
- Conscience, guilt, shame, and empathy are now possible and even likely (but can also be faked).
- Your deity is seen as a personified, anthropomorphic, named being who is focused on justice.
- You take religious metaphors, stories and symbolism literally.

Challenges

Although this stage is far less self-centered, it is still focused on your own needs. Financial strain, work stress and other situations that cause scarcity can pull you back to this stage. Fear of loss reigns supreme along with the fear of not having your needs met. There can be a lot of guilt, regret and shame in this stage when reflecting on your past actions. If there are people you need to apologize to, this is a good time to do it.

TASKS

☐ **Connect to others** - find ways to help others fulfill their needs.

Connect to yourself...

☐ Attend to your needs.

☐ Reflect on your past when you find patterns affecting you today.

☐ Define your value set / beliefs / ideologies and put it into practice.

Connect to your money...

☐ Solidify your savings engine.

☐ If you are not yet out of debt, double down on your efforts.

☐ If you are debt free (good job!), think about the funds you will need in the future and save, save, save.

> ### Resources
>
> - Your religious text(s) of choice
> - *Principles* by Ray Dalio
> - *The Jordan Harbinger Show* Podcast
> - Writings and speeches by His Holiness The Dalai Lama

Questions To Fuel Your Thinking

- Are there situations when you used others to fulfill your own needs, without regard to theirs? How would you handle those situations differently?

- What are you feeling?

- Who do you need to apologize to? Can you reach out to them?

- Can you let go of your past now and move forward?

- How do you currently prioritize your needs over or under the needs of others? Would you like to change that in order to find balance? Do you prioritize others too much above yourself? Or do you prioritize yourself too much above others? What should your principles be for prioritizing your needs and the needs of those you care about?

- What, according to your religion or other sources, should be the guiding principles of your life? Do you agree with those? How would you edit them for YOUR life?

Stage Five: I Am My Value Set / Ideology / Religion / Beliefs

CHARACTERISTICS

- You define yourself based on a set of social, moral, political and religious values.
- You have a strong affinity for laws and ethical codes.
- Anything that conflicts with your ideology is ignored or attacked.
- When you see or hear something that conflicts with your ideology, you feel offended or angry.
- You see people with other ideologies as lesser or lower than you, or not human at all, or deserving of bad things.

CHALLENGES

This stage is very challenging because you feel offended and shocked more often than you feel anything else. And just when you think you are beyond this, there is nothing like a good election, news program or religious retreat to pull you back into your ideology. Reading headlines focused on defending and attacking ideologies (political, religious or otherwise) will keep you in this stage far longer than is necessary and will only exacerbate the negatives of this stage. While it is important to HAVE an ideology just to get through your day and make good choices, it is more important to avoid swinging it at everyone who may feel differently. The biggest challenge in this stage is to have and evolve an ideology but to keep it on the shelf instead of wearing it. Your ideology is there for reference, but you are so much more.

Tasks

Connect to yourself...

☐ Read about other ideologies - political, social, religious, etc.

☐ Resist the urge to attack or be rude to others who think differently than you. It may feel justified right now but will be yet one more thing you will have to forgive yourself for in later stages.

☐ Return to your principles... based on new experiences, do they need to be updated?

☐ Consider that you HAVE an ideology, but you are so much more.

☐ **Connect to others** - see their humanity through their ideology. (Understand that if they are also in this stage, they may attack or ignore you if you try to sway them. So do not try to sway them, or anyone else. You will be ignored, or attacked and will ultimately not sway anyone.)

Don't forget to:

☐ Stay connected to your body, movement, sexuality, health, energy and feelings.

☐ Stay connected to your money - resist debt in any form, maintain your savings engine and save for your dreams.

☐ Maintain your needs.

☐ Update your principles and ideology as new experiences shape you.

> **RESOURCES**
>
> - The political platforms of each major party in your country (yes, all of them) and those of other countries
> - Every religious text you can find (*The Bible, The Torah, The Qur'an, The Bhagavad Gita, The Tao Te Ching, The Dhammapada*, etc)
> - *The Four Agreements* by Don Miguel Ruiz

Questions To Fuel Your Thinking

- What aspects or big ideas or underlying truths from other religious texts, other political platforms and other ways of thinking do you connect with?

- Are there some changes you would like to make to update your own principles or ideologies?

- Could you reframe your ideology further around principles instead of specific issues?

- If you are not your ideology, not your needs, not your experiences…. what are you? Are you ready to maybe not know for a while?

Stage Six: To Each Their Own (I Am My Ideology And Others Are Theirs)

CHARACTERISTICS

- You can put yourself in other people's shoes and feel what it is like to be them. You can see why they would have a different ideology and what that would be.
- You can consider other ideologies without feeling like yours is being attacked, and without attacking others.
- You reflect on the inconsistencies and complexities of your ideologies and are comfortable with them.
- ...But you think there might be something more; a larger perspective or truth that you are missing.

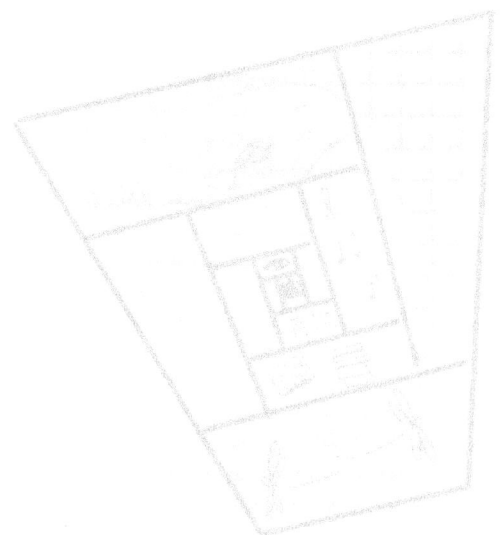

CHALLENGES

There are far fewer challenges in this stage. You feel much happier with your life. Although you are still defined by your ideology, you are living in a bit of a fantasy world in thinking that your ideology is perfect, or that the inconsistencies are OK. Many adults stay very happily in this stage for life. The treadmill of work, sleep, work, sleep can be a lifelong endeavor and can feel purposeful if you have work that you love. If however, you, like most, feel that call to figure out the truth of your self and your life and to design a life of peace, joy, excitement, or anything else you want... Complete this stage and proceed to stage seven.

TASKS

Connect to yourself...

☐ Return to your own ideology: Detail the cracks, the inconsistencies, hypocrisies and conflicts.

☐ Look in the mirror and see the person causing 99% of all your problems.

☐ Forgive and accept yourself as human.

☐ **Connect to your body** - Set specific, measurable, and attainable goals with near term milestones.

☐ **Connect to your heart** - See that you are worthy of your own love and of the infinite love inside you.

Connect to others...

☐ See everyone as a reflection of some aspect of yourself.

☐ Connect to the divine light inside them.

☐ Forgive and accept others as human.

☐ Forgive and accept the existence of aspects of society that you previously rejected (groups of people, norms, standards, societal rules, etc).

Don't forget to:

☐ Stay connected to your body, movement, sexuality, health, energy and feelings.

☐ Stay connected to your money - resist debt in any form, maintain your savings engine and save for your dreams.

☐ Maintain your needs.

☐ Update your principles and ideology as new experiences shape you.

☐ Consider if you are ready to go on the journey that the next few steps entail.

☐ Do not proceed to Stage Seven until you have addressed forgiveness of yourself and others.

Resources

- *The Four Hour Body* by Tim Ferriss
- *Life Lessons* by Elisabeth Kubler-Ross, M.D. and David Kessler
- *Peaks and Valleys* by Spenser Johnson
- *Who Moved My Cheese* by Spencer Johnson
- *Walden* by Henry David Thoreau
- *Civil Disobedience* by Henry David Thoreau
- *Vagabonding* by Rolf Potts
- Speeches by KRS—One (search YouTube for videos uploaded by audiences)

Questions To Fuel Your Thinking

- List out the problems you currently face - how are you responsible for them? How can you take responsibility for changing them?

- What do you need to forgive yourself for?

- What do you need to forgive others for?

- What is it to forgive?

- How much money can you save up and how fast?

- What is it to feel worthy of your own love?

- What is it to connect with others on all levels - intellectual, heart, soul, truth, energy?

Stage Seven: Questioning Everything

Characteristics

- In an effort to understand what you are missing, you question everything.
- You realize that happiness cannot be found in the outside world. This is a source of disappointment but also of hope.
- You reject ALL ideologies for now, while you question them.
- Previous doubts become meaningful, actionable questions.
- Sometimes you feel lonely because others are still devoted to their ideologies and they don't understand why you are questioning it.
- You tend to question and undertake this stage in private because of the risk of being alienated from your friends and/or communities.

Challenges

DO NOT MAKE ANY DRASTIC CHANGES IN THIS STAGE! Your best course is to try and not do anything stupid during this phase - no major purchases, no new debt, no job changes, no relationship changes, ... until you make it to Stage Eight and have stability and a clearer mind. Stage Seven is all about tearing down everything that everyone else told you life should be and what you should do, questioning that, and deciding for yourself what you want your self and your life to be. You will want to define that clearly before you make any major changes other than nutrition, exercise, and meditation or prayer. Get through this stage as fast as you can but COMPLETE it so that you will not be pulled back here very often.

This is by far the hardest stage. If you have baggage from your childhood, or past experiences that you have not addressed before, this is where you will have to deal with it. If you can be a bit of a hermit during this stage you may thank yourself later.

This stage is also where you are most likely to be depressed and to feel hopeless or that life is pointless. Existential crises are normal here. Understand that this is a natural part of your development and it will pass with time and effort.

Because of the existential nature of this stage, it is more important than ever to maintain connection to your mind, body, self, others, needs, etc. Keep up your efforts to save money, improve your nutrition, maintain some kind of exercise or movement, and all the other skills you have gathered so far.

TASKS

☐ **Connect to your faith** - Understand that questioning your religion is deep exploration that can bring you closer to the divine.

☐ **Question everything**... Religious teachings, social standards, political stances, societal norms, life choices, your lifestyle, your work...(Do not try to make others join you in this questioning if they are not ready. This is YOUR journey, not theirs.)

Connect to yourself...

☐ Practice being mindful of your thoughts and feelings.

☐ Identify the beliefs about yourself, your life, others and your world put into your mind by your parents, friends, and society. Decide if they are right for you.

☐ Identify your own behaviors that are sabotaging you (refresh your efforts to find and break negative patterns from Stage Four)

☐ Dig deep to uncover your own pain from the past and work through it.

☐ Decide who and what you want to be - more caring? Complete unto yourself? At peace? Quiet your mind and ask how you can achieve these in a healthy way.

☐ **Connect to the infinite silence / divine.**

Don't forget to:

☐ Stay connected to your body, movement, sexuality, health, energy and feelings.

☐ Stay connected to your money - resist debt in any form, maintain your savings engine and save for your dreams.

☐ Maintain your needs.

☐ Update your principles and ideology as new experiences shape you.

☐ See and accept your own humanity and the humanity of others.

Resources

- *Don't Sweat The Small Stuff* by Richard Carlson, Ph.D.
- *How To Stop Worrying and Start Living* by Dale Carnegie
- *Play It Away* by Charlie Hoehn
- *Sway* by Ori Brafman and Rom Brafman
- *The Subtle Art Of Not Giving A F*ck* by Mark Manson
- The Tony Robbins Podcast
- *The Tim Ferriss Show* Podcast
- *Letters From A Stoic* by Seneca
- *The Obstacle Is The Way* by Ryan Holiday

Questions To Fuel Your Thinking

- How can you be more kind to yourself?

- What unfinished business do you have? Baggage, limiting beliefs, forgiveness?

- Who do you want to be?

- What do you want your life to FEEL like?

- Can you sense deep in yourself, the infinite peace that the universe/divine put inside you? Can you connect to that?

- What survived your questioning? What are the right beliefs, principles, standards, work and lifestyles for YOU right now?

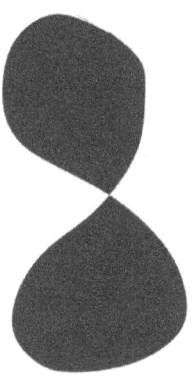

Stage Eight: I Am A Child Of The Universe/Divine

Characteristics

- You cycle through several belief sets trying to find one that fits and then eventually, instead of rejecting all ideologies, you actively examine them to find what parts are true.
- You see connections and relationships between ideologies.
- You see the interdependent truth at the heart of all ideologies and use THAT to anchor yourself.
- You surrender to not knowing all the answers.

Challenges

In this stage it it now much safer to begin designing your ideal life and making changes. Think through those changes carefully. Take your time so that you might be able to implement your ideal life more efficiently and effectively.

TASKS

☐ **Connect to the universal truth.**

☐ **Connect to the Silent Observer.**

☐ **Connect to your reality** - design your future.

☐ **Connect to your purpose** - identify it.

☐ **Connect to others** - can you see their truth now? Can you see their heart? Can you see their humanity? Can you see what stage they are in at the moment? Practice!

Don't forget to:

☐ Stay connected to your body - movement, feelings, energy, sexuality, health.

☐ Stay connected to your money - resist debt in any form, maintain your savings engine and save for your dreams.

☐ Maintain your needs.

☐ Update your principles and ideology as new experiences shape you.

☐ See and accept your own humanity and the humanity of others.

☐ Question everything and seek the honest truth, even if it does not agree with your current ideologies or what you would hope is the truth.

☐ Connect to the infinite peace/divine inside you.

QUESTIONS TO FUEL YOUR THINKING

- With any decision you make, what is the emotional root of this choice? Fear? Greed? Joy? Purpose? Be honest with yourself. Avoid decisions based on negative emotions.

- What do you want your life to be? What do you want to FEEL?

- What is your purpose here? What is your unique contribution to this world?

RESOURCES

- *The War of Art* By Steven Pressfield
- *The 4 Hour Work Week* by Tim Ferriss
- *Wherever You Go There You Are* by Jon Kabat-Zinn
- *The Crossroads of Should and Must* by Elle Luna
- *The Art of Everyday Ecstasy* by Margot Anand
- *Dangerous Personalities* by Joe Navarro
- *The Laws Of Human Nature* by Robert Greene

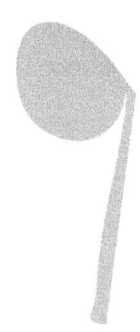

Stage Nine: I Am A Consciousness Trapped In This Body

CHARACTERISTICS

- You see religions, people, ideologies, places, and everything as one coherent whole with love at the heart of it all.
- You see that there is no self - you are a consciousness separate from your body and can feel the differences between your physical self and your internal consciousness.
- You do not blame anyone for anything happening in your own life.
- You have a sense of your purpose or mission.

CHALLENGES

The major challenge of this stage is to cultivate presence in the NOW. This moment, not the past or the future. It is a good challenge to have, but harder than it sounds. This stage is a beautiful and purpose filled place. The joy of acting on your newfound purpose is overwhelming. At the same time, you can feel guilty about this amazing life you are building. You can feel humbled by this gift of insight and connection. But you cannot end the suffering of others by joining them. You CAN, however, offer peace, joy and the example of a path towards a better life. That being said, do not preach. Just live your joy and shine bright.

TASKS

☐ **Connect to this moment.**

☐ **Connect to your intuition.**

☐ **Connect to your purpose** - make a plan.

☐ **Connect to your intellect** - gather the skills and knowledge you need to forward your purpose.

☐ **Form a more complete connection to your partner.**

Don't forget to:

☐ Stay connected to your body - movement, feelings, energy, sexuality, health.

☐ Stay connected to your money - resist debt in any form, maintain your savings engine and save for your dreams.

☐ Maintain your needs.

☐ Update your principles and ideology as new experiences shape you.

☐ See and accept your own truth and humanity and that of others.

☐ Question everything and seek the honest truth, even if it does not agree with your current ideologies or what you would hope is the truth.

☐ Connect to the infinite peace/divine and silent observer inside you.

RESOURCES

- *The Power of Now* by Eckhart Tolle
- *The First Three Minutes* by Steven Weinberg
- *Guide To Intuitive Healing* by Judith Orloff M.D.
- *REIKI: A Comprehensive Guide* by Pamela Miles
- *Fluent Forever* by Gabriel Wyner

QUESTIONS TO FUEL YOUR THINKING

- Can you be fully present NOW?

- Can you trust your intuition? What does it tell you?

- How can you manifest your purpose in this world? What skills and knowledge do you need?

- Can you feel the infinite peace and joy inside you? Can you let it flow out of you?

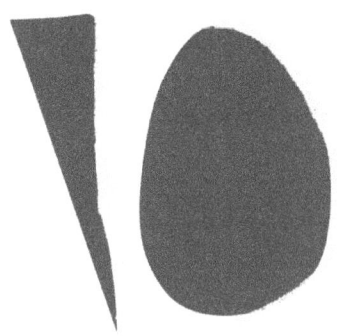

Stage Ten: I Am The ONE Consciousness

CHARACTERISTICS

- You realize that there is only one consciousness. You are an extension of that, as is everyone and everything else.
- You trust your intuition and begin to listen to it more often, training it to tell you what you need to know.
- You live in the moment, not worrying about the future or reliving the past.

CHALLENGES

The biggest challenge in this stage is maintaining the feeling of oneness that you have with everyone and everything. If you try to maintain it, it fades away. You have to not try, and just be in the now, feeling it, flowing in the moment. Be cognizant of how easily you can be pulled back around the cycle into other stages.

TASKS

☐ **Connect to higher wisdom**.

☐ **Connect to the oneness and your influence**.

☐ **Recognize the triggers** that take you out of this stage and make efforts to guard your environment accordingly.

Don't forget to:

☐ Stay connected to this moment.

☐ Stay connected to your intuition, the infinite peace/divine and silent observer inside you.

☐ Stay connected to your energy, body, feelings, sexuality, health, money, needs, humanity and truth.

☐ Update your principles and ideology as new experiences shape you.

> ### Resources
>
> - *Biocentrism* by Robert Lanza, MD
> - *The Wim Hof Method* (video series)

Questions To Fuel Your Thinking

- What do you want for your life right now? Why?

- What do you feel compelled to do? Is it compelling or impulse?

- What does the energy inside you feel like? Where in your body do you feel it? How does it feel differently in different parts of your body?

- What are the triggers that pull you back around the cycle?

- What practices, guidelines, and processes can you put in place to safeguard your time in this stage?

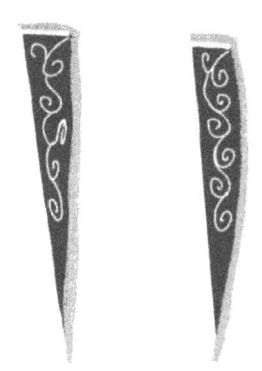

Stage Eleven: I Am The One Consciousness & The Physical Manifestation Simultaneously And There Is No Difference

Characteristics

- You feel the one consciousness, here in this human body, experiencing what it is like to be human - to ignore your humanity would be to miss out on the experience.
- You are matter and energy at the same time. You can consciously choose to experience the moment as either one, or both.
- There is no difference between the energy and the physical.
- You can consciously influence your reality to actively build an ideal life for yourself and alter it as your ideal evolves.
- You live in purpose, peace and joy.
- You connect deeply with yourself, your loved ones, friends and strangers.
- You exude a peace and joy that make people want to be near you.

Challenges

Maintenance, Maintenance, Maintenance. There is a lot to maintain at this point: your needs, your ideology, your experiences, your sense of connectedness and oneness. Once you have tasted this stage, you may find yourself crafting a life for yourself that will let you spend as much time here as possible. That ideal life will look very different for each of us. As you create space for further (yes, further!) development, you can begin to experiment with actively creating complete connection to yourself, your world, others, etc. Complete connection can help you to return to this stage and stay there as long as possible. In addition to actively creating complete connection, allow your naturally connected state to exist by removing whatever may be covering it up and blocking it. Actively seek complete connection, and simultaneously relax and allow that complete connection to happen.

TASKS

☐ **Connect to your reality.**

☐ Actively and consciously **design and create your ideal life** and your ideal self. Live in your purpose with peace and joy.

☐ **Recognize** when you are cycling through the stages again. Remember that life will take you around the circle many times but YOU are in control of how much time you spend in each stage.

☐ **Ripples in the water** - the strong, consistent signal wins.

☐ **Enjoy your human existence** in all of its most basic aspects as well as its more subtle complexities.

☐ **Seek complete connection** with yourself, with others, with this moment, your life at large, your money, your purpose, etc.

Don't forget to:

☐ Stay connected to this moment.

☐ Stay connected to your intuition, the infinite peace/divine and silent observer inside you.

☐ Stay connected to your energy, body, feelings, sexuality, health, money, needs, humanity and truth in this moment.

☐ Update your principles and ideology as new experiences shape you.

Resources

- This book! - *Purna Asatti*
- *On Life And Being Human* Podcast by Kathryn Colleen (send in your questions).

Questions To Fuel Your Thinking

- What daily and/or weekly practices can you put in place to process experiences, understand your changing needs and meet them, understand your evolving ideologies and maintain perspective?

- What regular practices can you put in place to create and maintain complete connection to yourself? To others? To this moment? To this world? To the oneness?

- Can you craft an efficient and effective daily routine that helps you spend the maximum time possible in this stage? What would that look like?

Questions, Answers And Additional Resources

Do you have questions about what you have read here? Go to KathrynColleen.com and send in your questions. Kathryn will answer you back as quickly as possible and may include your question on the podcast or blog.

Also at KathrynColleen.com, you will find:

- Links to the full edition of the book, which includes specific exercises and how-to for each task plus art and poetry for a different perspective on each stage.

- The music album, *Purna Asatti - Music For Complete Connection*, that accompanies this book

- The podcast, *On Life And Being Human*, where many of your questions may be answered.

- Other books, albums, essays and art by Kathryn Colleen.

- And more!

About The Author

Dr. Amy "Kathryn Colleen" Messegee is an American-born author, composer and artist better known for her foundational work: Purna Asatti, a process and practice that uses connection to self, others and every aspect of your life for managing challenges and accelerating self development.

Her summer job at 16 was doing scientific research at NASA. Before her 25th birthday she earned her Ph.D in Mathematics and was speaking to conferences on human reasoning and how to make the infinite finite. A hyper-polymath, her career has enjoyed a ride through…

- academia (as a professor of Mathematics),
- defense technology (as a Scientist, CTO, and DARPA Program Manager),
- online media (as founder of a business website and video podcast with a reach of 1.3 million),
- venture capital (advising VC firms on evaluating technologies and reading the founders for their true intent),
- private education (as founder of a local network of elite tutors and private instructors),
- and her current passion: human connection and energy work.

In each of these, the theme is always the same: aggregating seemingly unrelated perspectives to distill a new approach for accelerated results. She has published many books, hundreds of articles and papers, dozens of unique art pieces and released multiple albums.

She is known for taking only four students each year but influences and leads thousands around the world in more than 70 countries through speaking, writing, music, art and podcasts.

She is a Reiki Master Practitioner/Teacher and is travel-proficient in nine languages which she is learning simultaneously so she can live out her dream of traveling the world, speaking at pop up events and aggregating insight on life, the universe and being human.

See **KathrynColleen.com** for more information, books, articles, music, podcasts, and resources.

www.ingramcontent.com/pod-product-compliance
Lightning Source LLC
Chambersburg PA
CBHW081354040426
42450CB00016B/3434